How Do Our Eyes See?

Carol Ballard

RSVP

RAINTREE
STECK-VAUGHN
PUBLISHERS
The Steck-Vaughn Company

Austin, Texas

How Your Body Works

How Do Our Eyes See?

How Do Our Ears Hear?

How Do We Taste and Smell?

How Do We Feel and Touch?

How Do We Think?

How Do We Move?

Published by Raintree Steck-Vaughn Publishers, an imprint of Steck-Vaughn Company

Library of Congress Cataloging-in-Publication Data
Ballard, Carol.
How Do Our Eyes See? / Carol Ballard.
p.   cm.—(How Your Body Works)
Includes bibliographical references and index.
Summary: A basic introduction to how our bodies see, exploring such topics as light and dark, color, and glasses.
ISBN 0-8172-4736-X
1. Vision—Juvenile literature.
[1. Vision. 2. Eye. 3. Senses and sensation.]
I. Title. II. Series.
QP475.7.B35   1998
612.8'4—dc21   97-7708

Printed in Italy. Bound in the United States.
1 2 3 4 5 6 7 8 9 0 02 01 00 99 98

Picture Acknowledgments
The author and publishers thank the following for use of their photographs:
Chapel Studios 4, 5 (top), 7, 22; Chris Fairclough *cover,* 13, 21, 28; Gary Fry/RNIB 27; Robert Harding 4, 16; Reflections 17; Tony Stone *title page,* 19; Zefa *contents page,* 5, 18, 20, 23, and 29.
The remaining pictures are from the Wayland Picture Library.
Illustrations by Kevin Jones Associates and Michael Courtney

Contents

Eyes

Our eyes are very important. We use them to find out about the world around us.

▲

It would be hard to enjoy television if we could not see the screen.

Our eyes help keep us safe. We use them to look for traffic before we cross the road. We also use our eyes so we don't bump into things.

▲

◄ We use our eyes to watch for warning signs and signals.

Our eyes allow us to enjoy the world we live in. If we look carefully, we can see tiny animals and plants, beautiful countryside, and wonderful views. In cities we often walk past interesting buildings without noticing them. This book will tell you more about your eyes and how they work.

▲
◀ Our eyes enable us to see to read, to write, and to use a computer.

Look at Your Eyes

When you look at your eyes, you can see that they are made up of many parts.

Eyebrows are ridges of skin with short, flat hairs attached. They keep dust and sweat out of the eyes.

6

▲
A camel's long eyelashes help protect its eyes from sand and bright sunlight.

Eyelids and eyelashes prevent dust and dirt from getting in the eyes. Eyelids keep the eyes moist. When you blink, tear fluid is spread over the surface of your eyes.

◀ Members of a family often have eyes of the same color.

The white part of the eye is called the **sclera**. At the center of the eye, the sclera is clear, so light can pass through it. This clear part is called the **cornea**.

The colored part of the eye is called the **iris**. At the center of each eye is a black circle called the **pupil**. This is a hole that lets light into the eye.

The color of the iris depends on the amount of **pigment** in it. Brown eyes have a lot of pigment, blue eyes have less.

▼

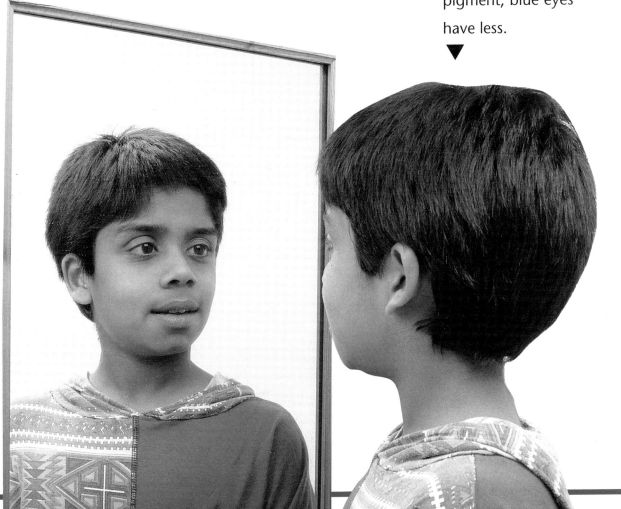

Inside an Eye

Your eye is like a soft, hollow ball filled with liquid and jelly. Inside the eye the ball is divided into two parts called chambers. The small front chamber is filled with a watery liquid. The other larger chamber is filled with a soft jelly. The jelly and the liquid make the eyes solid and shaped like a ball.

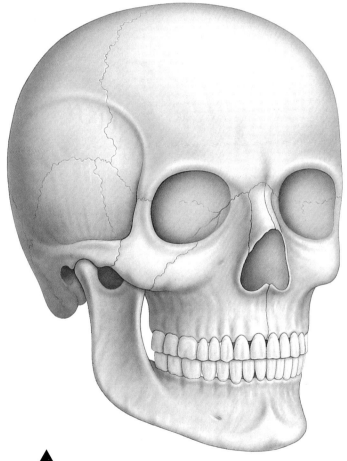

▲

Each eyeball lies inside a bony hollow in the skull. These hollows are strong and protect the eyes from injury.

Between the two chambers is a clear disk called the **lens**. This is held in place by rings of muscles.

At the back of the eye is a layer called the **retina**.
The lens bends the light as it enters the eye
to **focus** on the retina. The retina reacts
when light hits it and sends
a message along the
optic nerve to
the brain.

skull bone

chamber filled
with jelly

chamber
filled with
liquid

retina

optic nerve

9

cornea

pupil

Diagram of the
inside of an eye ▶

lens

muscles

How Do Eyes Work?

We need light in order to see. Imagine you are looking at a tree. Light from the sun falls on the tree. It bounces off the tree and travels to your eyes. Light passes through the cornea, which bends it a little. It then passes through the front chamber and pupil to the lens. As the light rays pass through the lens, they are bent even more. They then pass through the back chamber of your eye to the retina.

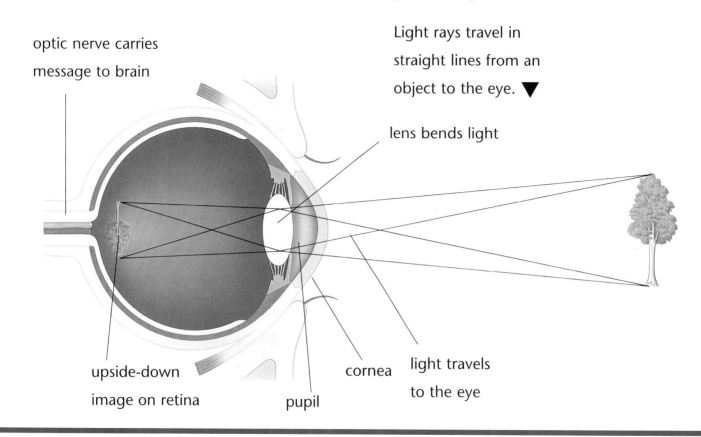

optic nerve carries
message to brain

Light rays travel in
straight lines from an
object to the eye. ▼

lens bends light

upside-down
image on retina

cornea

pupil

light travels
to the eye

When light lands on the retina, an **image** of the tree is formed. Because the lens bends the light, the image on the retina is upside-down.

The retinas of both eyes send messages about the tree to the brain. The brain sorts out the messages and you "see" the tree. All this happens so quickly that it seems to take no time at all.

Your eye is like a ▶ camera. Light passes through a hole and is bent by a lens. A picture is formed at the back of the eye. In a camera the picture is on a film.

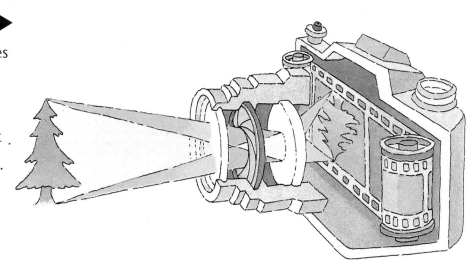

Light and Dark

We can see clearly only if the right amount of light enters our eyes. If the light is too bright, we scrunch our faces up. This pulls our eyelids closer together and shuts out some of the light.

▲
Cats' eyes have an extra layer inside. They reflect any light that shines on them, so they seem to glow in the dark.

The size of the pupils controls how much light enters the eyes. In bright light the pupils close until they are just a tiny hole. This keeps out a lot of light. In dim light the pupils open wide to let in as much light as possible.

◀ Reflective strips on this girl's backpack and arm will help drivers see her in the dark.

Look carefully at your eyes in a mirror. Notice the size of your pupils. Now shut your eyes and cover them with your hands. Count slowly to one hundred. Open your eyes and look quickly into the mirror. Now your pupils have become larger, to let in more light.

13

▲
Pupils are large in
dim light.

▲
We can see clearly in
normal light.

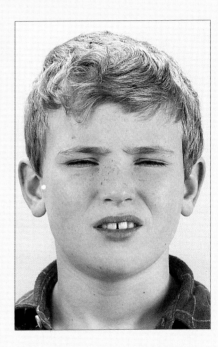

▲
We scrunch our eyes up in
bright light.

Near, Far, and Wide

You can judge distances and shapes because you have two eyes. When you look at something, each eye has a slightly different view of it and sends a different message to your brain. Your brain puts the two messages together to give you the whole picture.

When you look at a cube like this, your left eye sees more of the red side and your right eye sees more of the green side. The brain puts this information together and you get a balanced view. ▼

To see objects at different distances, each lens has to change its shape. To see close objects, each lens becomes fatter. To see distant objects, each lens becomes thinner.

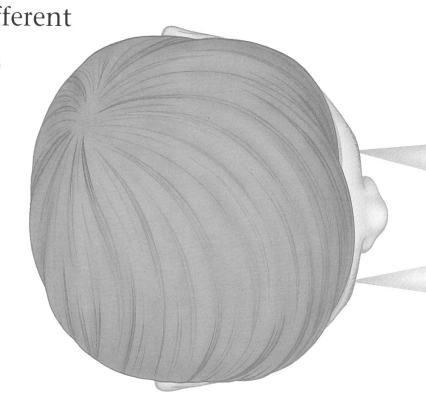

To see things at the side and behind, we have to turn our heads. To find out how far to the side you can see, look straight ahead at something. First, get a friend to stand behind you and then slowly walk around you in a circle. Keep staring straight ahead, and tell your friend to stop when you can see him or her.

▲

A hawk's eyes are at the front of its head so it can find its prey ahead. A rabbit's eyes are on the sides of its head so it has an all-around view of any danger.

Seeing in Color

The retina is made up of millions of **cells**. There are two types of cells in the retina that react to light. They are called rods and cones.

Rods **detect** the amount of light that lands on them. Cones detect the color of the light that lands on them. When you look at a toy, the rods tell the brain how light or dark the toy is. The cones tell the brain what color the toy is.

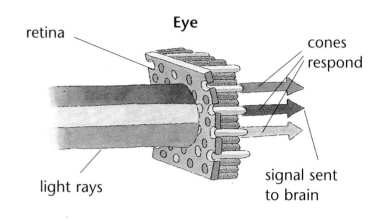

Eye

retina

cones respond

light rays

signal sent to brain

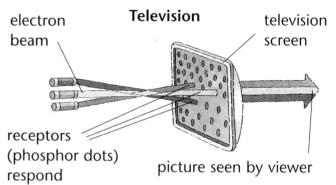

electron beam

Television

television screen

receptors (phosphor dots) respond

picture seen by viewer

▲

Each retina is like a television screen. Electronic receptors in television screens detect red, green, or blue light.

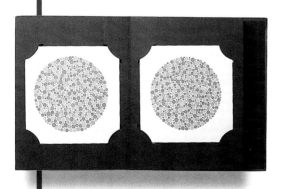

◄ People who are color-blind may not see the numbers 29 and 57 among the dots.

There are three types of cone cells. Each cone cell reacts to just one of the primary colors of light— red, green, or blue. If you look at a red apple, the red cone cells react but the blue and green cone cells do not.

People who cannot see a full range of colors are color-blind. To someone who is red-green color-blind, a red apple and green grass would look like the same color.

This boy is having ▶ his eyes tested for color-blindness.

Do You Need Glasses?

People wear glasses for different reasons. Nearsighted people can see objects that are close to them, but objects far away from them are blurred. Their glasses help them see distant objects more clearly.

▲
You should be able to read a book easily if you hold it about 12 in. (30 cm.) away from your eyes.

Farsighted people can see objects that are far away easily, but find it hard to see things that are close to them.

Their glasses help them see close objects more clearly.

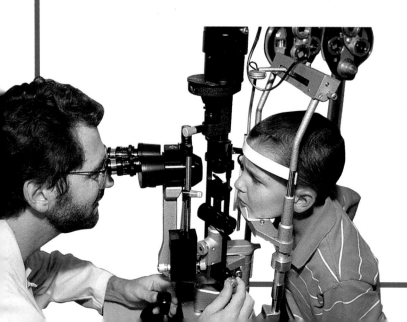

◀ An **optometrist** checks to see that this child's eyes are healthy.

Some children can see clearly but need to wear glasses to correct other eye problems. Glasses can sometimes help if a child's eyes do not work together or if they are not developing properly.

Can you read a book and see the computer screen clearly? If not, you may need glasses. Tell an adult so that an eye exam can be arranged.

▼

A Visit to the Optometrist

Katie is going to the optometrist to have her eyes tested. To make sure she gets the right glasses, the optometrist asks her if any of her family wears glasses, if she has eye problems, or if she is taking any medicine. The optometrist also asks her if she has had any headaches.

Contact lenses are tiny lenses that fit on the front of each eye. They need careful cleaning.

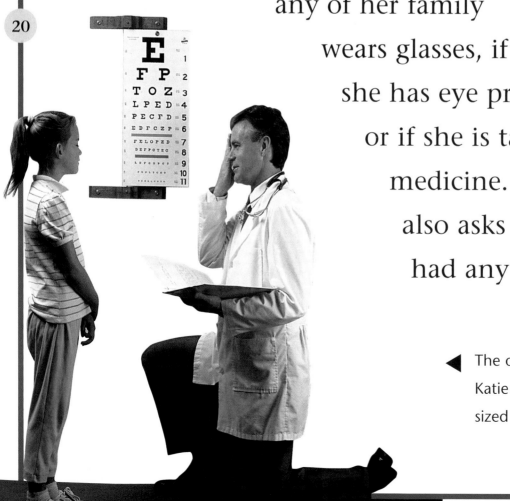

◀ The optometrist checks if Katie can read the different-sized letters on the chart.

The optometrist asks Katie to read some letters on a chart. First, she reads it with both eyes. Then, the optometrist covers one eye, and Katie reads the chart, with each eye. He shines a light into Katie's eyes to look inside them and check the retina at the back of each eye.

Once the optometrist has finished all his tests, he knows which lenses Katie needs to help her see clearly.

An optometrist takes ▶ measurements to make sure that this girl's glasses will fit properly.

21

As You Grow

When they are first born, babies cannot see tiny objects or a lot of detail. After a few months, their eyes can follow a moving toy or person. Babies do not start to see really clearly until they are about two years old.

22

Young children may need glasses to help them see. They cannot read letters, and some are too young to talk, so optometrists use cards with patterns and pictures to test their eyesight.

▲ People often need more than one pair of glasses as they get older, but they can wear only one at a time!

◄ A baby can see movements and shapes but cannot see details clearly.

Many children start to wear glasses during their first years at school. Some will need to wear them for the rest of their lives. Others will need to wear them for just a few years until the problem is corrected.

As they get older, many adults find that they need to wear glasses to help them read and to see objects far away. To avoid changing glasses all the time, they wear special lenses called bifocals. ▼

Optical Illusions

Sometimes the brain gets confused about what it sees. The pictures on this page are called optical illusions. Each picture can be seen two ways. Usually the brain uses information from the eyes and memory to make sense of what you are looking at, but sometimes the brain will be wrong.

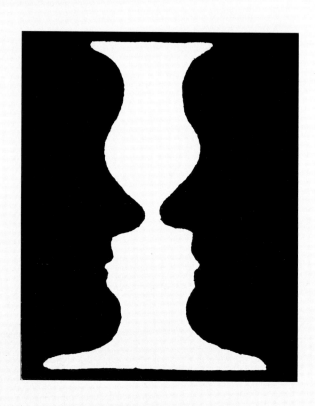

What do you see? Two black faces or one white candlestick? A young girl or an old witch? There are two images in each picture. Your eyes send all the information and your brain has to choose which you see.

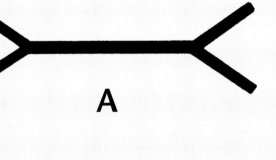

A

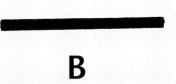

B

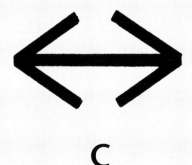

C

▲

Look carefully at these lines. Which do you think is longest, A, B, or C? Now measure them with a ruler. Surprised? The short, outside lines on A and C trick your brain. Those on A make the line look longer, and those on C make it look shorter.

25

▲

Put a strip of thin cardboard upright on the dotted line. Look at the bird and the cage. Gradually move your head closer to the page until your nose rests on the cardboard. What happens? Your brain gets a picture of a bird from your left eye and a picture of a cage from your right eye. It has to put the information together, so you see the bird inside the cage. (If you don't see the bird inside the cage, try a longer or shorter piece of cardboard.)

Blindness

For **blind** people to lead **independent** lives, they need special help.

With a guide dog, a blind person can go outside safely. Guide dogs are trained to guide their owners around obstacles such as lampposts.

The owner gives the dog instructions by pulling on its special harness.

◀ A guide dog can help a blind person move around safely.

There are many objects specially designed to help blind people lead ordinary lives.

Many blind people read by using a special alphabet called **braille**. A pattern of raised dots stands for each letter, and the letters are read by feeling the dots with one's fingers.

Instead of lights and signs, blind people often rely on sounds. They can tell the time by using a talking watch. A special clip on the side of a cup bleeps when liquid touches it, so the person knows when the cup is full. Blind people put things down in certain places so they know exactly where these things are the next time they want them.

This blind girl is reading a braille ▶ book. The machine in front of her is called a brailler, which she uses to type in braille.

27

Take Care of Your Eyes

A balanced diet provides the vitamins you need for healthy eyes.

It is important to take care of your eyes, whether or not you wear glasses. Here are some suggestions about how to keep your eyes healthy.

Computer and television screens can be bad for your eyes if you sit in front of them for a long time without a break. When watching television, try not to sit too close. It can be tempting to hold a book right under your nose when you read, but it is much better to hold it about 12 in. (30 cm) away.

You can get goggles made with your lenses so that you can see more easily when you are swimming.

If you wear glasses or contact lenses, visit the eye doctor regularly to have your eyes tested. Follow the doctor's advice, and wear your glasses when you are supposed to. If you play a lot of sports, wearing safety glasses can reduce the risk of an eye injury.

Goggles protect these children's eyes from the **glare** of the snow.

Glossary

blind Unable to see.

braille An alphabet of raised dots.

cells The millions of tiny building blocks that make up the body.

cornea The clear covering of the front of the eyeball.

detect To notice or pick up information.

focus To produce a clear image.

glare Bright, strong light.

image A picture made by light.

independent Able to look after oneself.

iris The colored part of the eye.

lens The clear disk that bends light to focus on the retina.

optic nerve The nerve that carries messages from the eye to the brain.

optometrist A doctor who is skilled in examining people's eyes.

pigment A substance in the iris that gives it color.

pupil The hole that lets light into the eye.

retina The back layer of the eye, which is sensitive to light.

sclera The thick white covering of most of the eyeball that gives the eye its rounded shape.

Books to Read

Greenaway, Theresa. *Ears & Eyes*. Head to Tail. Austin, TX: Raintree Steck-Vaughn, 1995.

Rauzon, Mark J. *Eyes & Ears*. New York: William Morrow & Co., Inc., 1994.

Index

32